The Gods of
East Wawanosh

Other Books by Marilyn Gear Pilling

FICTION

My Nose Is a Gherkin Pickle Gone Wrong (1996)
The Roseate Spoonbill of Happiness (2002)
On Huron's Shore (2014)

POETRY

The Field Next to Love (2002)
The Life of the Four Stomachs (2006)
Cleavage: A Life in Breasts (2007)
The Bones of the World Begin to Show (2009)
A Bee Garden (2013)
Estrangement (2017)

EDITED

Evenings on Paisley Avenue: Seven Hamilton Poets (2014)

Marilyn Gear Pilling

The Gods of
East Wawanosh

poems

Cormorant Books

The publisher gratefully acknowledges the support of the Canada Council for the Arts and
the Ontario Arts Council for its publishing program. We acknowledge the financial support
of the Government of Canada through the Canada Book Fund (CBF) for our publishing
activities, and the Government of Ontario through Ontario Creates, an agency of the
Ontario Ministry of Culture, and the Ontario Book Publishing Tax Credit Program.

LIBRARY AND ARCHIVES CANADA CATALOGUING IN PUBLICATION

Pilling, Marilyn Gear, author
The gods of East Wawanosh / Marilyn Gear Pilling.

Poems.
ISBN 978-1-77086-546-4 (softcover)

1. Huron (Ont. : County)—Poetry.
1. Title.

PS8581.¾365G63 2019   C811'.54   C2018-906270-3

Cover art and design: angeljohnguerra.com
Interior text design: Tannice Goddard, tannicegdesigns.ca
Printer: Sunville Printco

Printed and bound in Canada.

CORMORANT BOOKS INC.
260 SPADINA AVENUE, SUITE 502, TORONTO, ON M5T 2E4
www.cormorantbooks.com

This book is dedicated to my father, John Alexander Gear, 1918–1999
with thanks for his genes, his courage in adversity
and the love he felt and showed, not by saying but by doing

and to my mother, Jean McDowell Gear, 1918–1999
bless her Irish contrariness
her well developed sense of the ridiculous
and even her worst fear — that her elder daughter
would "grow up to be a writer"

Contents

I The Gods of East Wawanosh

II The Lives That Surround Us

The Gods of
East Wawanosh

I

The Gods of East Wawanosh

East Wawanosh is an area of Huron County, Ontario that is blessed by the ubiquitous Maitland River and her tributaries. It is named for Joshua Wawanosh, hereditary chief of the First Nations Chippewa.

i. Name on the Mailbox

Even after all this time, the old tin mailbox
at the end of the long lane still bears
the name of our ancestor, Armand McBurney.
Cedars along the narrow track
reach for my car, brushing, catching, scraping.
Grass trails its long fingers along
the undercarriage, a hollow sighing sound.
My father, my brother, never really
owned the farm. The farm owned
them, tugged at an unseen part of them
though they worked in the city.
The farm ruined both their marriages
inveigled both into her valleys, her fast flowing waters
her forest knolls, her layers and layers of
leaf bed, her sweet spring syrup.
I edge the car past the place where
pussy willows still show their soft
catkins in spring
past the big maple where the well
used to be, up the rise
to the low stone fence in front of the house
the front door we never used
the door above that opened into nowhere.
The gate to the outer yard is open.
For a half-second flash, I see a stranger, an old
stooped man with white hair.
He turns, he wears my brother's face.

ii. Leavings

Deep in the Dirty Thirties
      he puts on the worn
shirt given him by his brother-in-law
      who owns this farmhouse

and his one suit, holey though it be.
      Tiptoes into darkness
though at each step the stairs complain.
      Eats the cold leavings of yesterday's

porridge from the pot on top
      of the wood stove
sneaks through the back door
      before even the birds are up.

By the time he reaches the end
      of the long lane
his feet are damp with April melt.
      He neither looks back nor returns.

His young son, who will become
      my father,
has been left with his mother to live on
      porridge, thistles and stones.

My father will marry a woman
      whose favourite threat
will be that she'll leave him
      and never come back.

How do so many of us find them?
      These others
so willing to help us
      re-live the pain of our pasts.

iii Father

Your eyes the blue of roadside chicory,
my mother's eyes green and brown and yellow
like the odd marble in the toy box.

Her eyes looking at you.
There was not one thing right about you.
When I asked you a question she answered.

I spoke to you as she did, like the serf
in the history book, foot raised
"who had nothing to kick but his dog."

Cards from colleagues at Christmas, your birthday,
a mystery —
their number, the warmth of the messages.

A summer day I went with you for binder twine,
the Austin in creeper gear, grinding straight up
the gravel hill, I chipping away at you as she did.

You stopped the car at the top, broke into my talk,
your eyes — flash of chicory,
ripples above an invisible bottom:

You see me now with your mother's eyes.
When you grow up
you will see me with your own.

I saw the countryside from the top of that hill
toy farms
at the mercy of one sweep of your arm.

iv. "Birth of Son and Heir"

These the words you wrote in your journal
the day your son was born,
the words I read while sitting at your deathbed.

Today, I look at a black and white photo
of you, Father, taken in June '49
eight months after you wrote those words,

look at it and smell the sweet white blossoms
of the tall chestnut tree
that spread its efflorescent heaven

above the upstairs porch of the old city house
we rented back then.
Every lineament of your face, every double-jointed limb

relaxed, you sit beneath the blossoms, feeding your son.
There exists no word
adequate to describe the intensity of happiness

this photo records, as you raise the silver spoon
running over with pablum
to the open mouth of your heir.

Looking at this, who would believe the tragic story
the two of you would enact, enough
to erase from our memory what this photo portrays.

Yet it seems to be true, what Nabokov said
in old age — that linear time
is a mirage of human creation,

that there exists a greater time
in which all is still present,
even this.

v. The Plum

It looked like an overripe plum
in the middle of the back of his head
dark purple, a thumb-length above
the hairline. His baby hair would not lie flat
no matter how often
my mother wet it. Every day, I watched her
trying
to stick it down around the plum.

She told me never to touch it.

They brought him home the day I turned three.
Now, I am the only person alive
who knows how the plum looked.

Again and again, she told me the story.
The next day they brought him to me
I was so happy.
I stroked the back of his head and felt something.
Turned him over and there was this plum.
I felt sick.

Once, I did touch it. It was soft. Kept the slight
dent my finger made.
Once, I licked my finger
tried to stick down the baby hairs
watched them slowly rise around the plum.

*

For twenty-one months we lived inside
a web not quite strong enough
to hold us.
Then doctors sent my brother
to The Hospital for Sick Children.

They had to go to the base of the brain, said my mother
when she finally came home.

I saw men marching to the base of a mountain.
They carried axes and ropes
like men in a book I had.

*

A week before she died, she told me the story
one more time.

Her last three sentences new.

I stood at the one-way window.
In those days
the mother was not allowed into the room.
I saw his bandaged head, his white face.
He would look and look at the bare walls.
His lower lip would tremble
and he'd cry.

After ten days I was allowed in.
He wouldn't look at me.

I should have gone in. People wouldn't stand for that now.
But in those days
Doctors and Nurses were gods.

vi. The Stranger

My mother disappears with my brother
to The Hospital for Sick Children.
A stranger comes from
up home. A stranger whose name is
Aunt Edythe. I am four.
She walks me to school.
First days of kindergarten.

We have to pass the Witch's house.
I will not go past with my mother.
I cannot tell a stranger.
The witch
watches from her window.
She memorizes me for next time.

The chestnut trees used to be
my friends.
They stop speaking to me.

At school I cannot
make the yellow wool
go through
the holes in the chicken's wings.
Sudden the teacher.
Rap rap on my desk.
My heart
hits my throat, my ears.

The sobs at night
push my eyes hard from inside.
I think my eyes
will pop onto the soaked pillow.
My own room
a stranger.

vii. Eye of the Farm

In the depths of the valley
between the two farms
where willows overhung
water, where dragonflies
flittered and folded
where the creek bulged round,
was the swimming hole.
Above it, the log that allowed
us to cross or to lie
full length on its heat.
If ever there was a little heaven
for my brother and me
this was it.
Afternoons as long as a summer,
sun-warmed water shimmer
mirrored trees, long strands
of willow, everything imagined
as part of another world
we alone knew. Unique
smell of creek life
that stayed in our hair,
water spiders, crayfish
stonefish, families of leaves
that floated from upstream
passed beneath our log and
travelled on once we had
stopped them, warmed them
on the log, heard their stories
told them ours.
In the creek, the large flat stone
from which we launched ourselves
into water that allowed us
to enter its being, and belong.

viii. Call Answer

Two farms on high hills. Between them a valley and a creek.
To phone from one to the other
Long Distance,
our farm on the Wingham line, our uncle's on the Blyth.
Long Distance reserved, of course,
for a child up to his shoulder in the wringer washer
a man rammed into two dimensions by his bull.
Across the valley, Aunt Evelyn turned the radio to CKNX
each morning, kept the volume
loud enough
to hear the list of the local dead
from where she sat
wiping hen dirt and sticky straw
from the eggs. Aunt Evelyn, our mother's sister.
Our father the only one who could "raise" her.

If our mother needed to send her sister a message
he would gallop to the knoll in front of the old farmhouse.
You couldn't see their farm across the valley for the trees;
you trusted it was there.
He cupped his mouth, raised his chin, let loose a high keening wail
that rose and fell and woke the echoes.

E - vee-eeeeeeeeeeee.

          E - vee-eeeeeeeeeeeee.

If the Keening of the Name failed thrice, our father
began to yodel.
At the first note, my brother and I scuttled like centipedes
to the knoll, settled in for the performance.
Our mother stayed in the kitchen, viewed the racket as
an unseemly necessity.

Eh-e-vee-odel-eeee-yiiiip!

          Eh-e-vee-odel-eeee-yiiiip!

Every Christmas, our father insisted on having
Evelyn as his partner
for the card game Lost Heir; it featured four suits,
starred The Wrong Boy — scowling ruffian from Toronto —
and The Lost Heir — proud scion from Winnipeg.
Every year, our father and Aunt Evelyn
won most of the games.

One day my brother and I in our aunt's garden
heard our father's call
resound across the valley. We raced to the house
fetched Aunt Evelyn from the back kitchen,
Dad's calling.
She took off her apron and patted her housedress.
She paused before the sideboard's long horizontal
mirror and smoothed her hair.

E - vee-eeeeeeeeeeee.

She opened the screen door and walked on green grass to her knoll.
Cupped her hands and called her answer to the blue sky.

Yes, John, I'm here.

On her worn face the expression she wore on Christmas Day
when one of their cards — hers or our father's —
took the trick that gave them The Lost Heir
and the game.

ix. Carrots

Surprisingly often I think of those carrots,
how quickly they became flaccid and grey,
how every morning we returned to a fresh crop of the dead.
We had horses we rode everywhere,
tied them at night to a long rusty nail on the outhouse.
Mine was without bark, smooth and golden,
a short branch in the right place for a saddle horn.
Riding at speed, the dust clothed me,
the old West rose from the ditches.
My brother and cousin rode ordinary horses
rough with bark. We stole money from Aunt Evelyn's
lilac tree, leaf after leaf after leaf
counted and placed in stacks in the ancient billfold
we found in the attic where sleeping bats
hung until dusk.
Our aunt's garden was wide and long; the family
lived off its produce all winter.
She pickled, salted, dried, and put up preserves.
We waited
'til she'd gone to the back kitchen to wipe eggs
and listen in on the party line.
At a signal from me, we galloped down the hill,
in the hooves of our horses
outlaw thunder.
We plundered the carrots, ignored how they clung
to the dung-enriched soil,
yanked them from their warm, fertile beds.
Galloped to our hideout and dumped them.
Every day we took from those beds.
Took them crisp and orange and smelling of health.
Piled them higher and higher,
sat over our cache,
counted and counted and counted our gold.

x. Community Picnic, 1954

Mothers and children walked in the warm golden water
without hurting their feet
the river's floor hard and smooth here, for a whole mile.

Only our brother was tormented by the horseflies.
The excitement when ladies our mothers' age
looked us over and said, You must be Jean's girl,

or Evelyn's girl, or Edythe's girl. The fun of imitating them
later, for one another. At supper time
the dads and big boys arrived, signs of the hot day threshing

on their overalls and caps. The mothers fed us what they made
for funerals — soft white bread with crusts off
fillings of egg salad and canned salmon. Pies they'd made

with lard at six a.m. when they could stand the wood stove on —
harvest apple, sour red cherry, raspberry.
After supper baseball, horseshoes, three-leggèd races

in the wide shade cast by the bush. Dusk rose from the shadows
with the mosquitoes.
No one knew then that the horses would become unemployed

that the chickens and pigs and cows would become
lifers in long factories
that the Astrachans and Thomas Sweets and Melbas

would disappear along with the orchards that sheltered them.
No one knew that one by one
the farmhouses would lose their eyes and fall dumb

that the end-of-summer gathering of East Wawanosh folk,
as well as the gods who both
shattered and held their world together, would die before we did.

xi. Words Fell

Words fell from the highest
branches along with the apples
our father up there shaking and shaking
words and apples hitting the ground
with discrete thumps.
The new sun barely topped the high trees
of the nearby woods,
my brother and I on our knees
in the dew-wet grass
separated the bruised from the unscathed
placed them one by one
in bushel baskets
the apples, red on one side, green on the other
the words spittle-shined.
Half-split by the fall one word
spilled its seeds, hard and sharp
but the worm held back;
                    from within the word's
flesh, it moved its eyeless front end
as if to speak.
Before I could stop him, my brother
stretched out his arm, grabbed the half-split
word, swallowed it whole
and that
        was the beginning.

xii. August Visit to Great Aunt May

Always she took a long time to come to the door.
Always as we waited my grandmother said
May's slow, she's a cripple.
She had a contraption she pushed that kept her
upright. She opened the door.

Her chin-length white hair dead straight
parted on one side, held on the other by a black
bobby pin. One half of her face
lower than the other, one side of her mouth
sloppy. Long white whiskers

on her cheeks and chin. When she sees
our grandmother and our mother, me and my brother
she begins to cry.
I hang my head so as not to see
her shameful tears.

We sit in the messy kitchen.
Flies everywhere.
I dread the moment Great Aunt May
will look at me and speak; nothing is ever
expected of my brother.

When she does speak
my mother and grandmother
turn to look at me too.
Great Aunt May's speech is garbled
a word I've heard from my mother.

I look at the floor, cheeks and ears growing
larger, hotter. My mother translates.
Your Great Aunt wants a kiss.
This is something new. All of them stare at me.
Their mouths straight and narrow.

To bend and breathe the unfamiliar smell
to place my lips upon the hairy cheek
to be gripped, perhaps, by that speckled claw …

House flies eat from the dirty plates of the noon dinner.
Their busy front feet the only things that move.

xiii. Great Aunt May's Son

Eddie. Cockatoo hair, spikes of burning
orange. He led my little brother and me
to the unkempt side yard
where hapless hens missing half
their rusty feathers pecked at the dust.
He would have been in his thirties
those years of our summer visits.

He took us to the fence that kept the yard
safe from the field. The hens
emitted tenuous, intermittent plaints.
He dared us to touch the wire.
I said we were not allowed

to touch an electric fence.
He raised his chin and guffawed.
The sun blazed into his nostrils
lit a curtain of shining red-gold
hairs, the glints beyond.

He touched the wire himself.
Made a fist around it. Beckoned.

I took my brother's hand.
Tiptoed forward, stretched out an arm
touched a finger to the wire.
An invisible power knocked us back.
It took my breath, forced a wet shine
to my cheeks. My brother's face
crumpled like dry sand.

Eddie's guffaw so loud the hens scattered.
He slapped himself, bent double
stamped and danced on hen dung.
We carried our shame home. Never
spoke of it, even to one another.

xiv. Father, Waiting
East Wawanosh, late December 1942

Every time I stop at this crossroad in winter
there you are. Thumb out
waiting for the ride that will take you
to the city, to the beginning
of your working life.
Your thumb is blue, your ears are red
your jacket thin, your boots unlined.
Your slight frame shakes in the morgue-like cold,
a blue cold that enters bone.
You boarded for two years
to finish high school, lived on carrots
and peanut butter — did not touch either
ever again.
You adored the woman who adopted you
at seven. Followed her strictures
your whole life. Tried
to make your children follow them.
Your son lives now
in the wreck of farmhouse
you spent your life's weekends
keeping up. He has your disease
and now has lost
a layer of his limbic system.
Lives by your rules. Has become them.

xv. Anyways

Father. He doesn't believe it at first, asks for proof.
Finds his rimless reading glasses.
Tucks the small piece of foam
that disgusts his daughter
under the nosepiece that otherwise
cuts his flesh, bends to look at
the word
beneath which his daughter has placed her long fuchsia nail
has driven forty miles in the heat to place her long fuchsia nail.
Takes the brand new dictionary from her hands.

He'd drilled it into his children. Using
anyways instead of anyway
would mark them as somewhere above
beast of the field, but below
bright-eyed child, scrubbed and excelling at school.
Anyways was first cousin to *ain't,* its nose
running. It belonged with words like
pee and *belly,* and *me and him* used as subject
rather than object.
Anyways, and those other forbidden words
would bar his children from respect, ascent, prosperity.

A kind of faith, perhaps, went out of him
that hot, summer Sunday afternoon.
Before *anyways* got its promotion into the dictionary
he believed that there were certain absolutes by which
the world was governed, believed
he knew what they were.

He looked up, finally, at his firstborn.
Closed the dictionary and held it out to her.
Bowed his head.

That young self. The heat and rattle and steam of her
on the victory stove.
The pride that rose from her spout.

xvi. The Sabbath

Our father would not work on the Sabbath
   though the farm's broken fences
and bull thistles cried out to him
   and the Sabbath was half the time
available to him for farm work.
   Our father would not play
cards or Crokinole or even
   cut my brother's hair on the Sabbath.
My brother and I mocked him for it.

Our father bowed his head to bless
   our Sunday suppers
of tomatoes, ham and bread.
   I stared straight ahead
forced my eyes wide open
   as he prayed, allowed them
not one blink although
   they stung and stung and finally
gave up tears.

xvii. The Gods of East Wawanosh

We have eaten July dust on the way.
We have half-carried my father up the hill.
On her knees now, pulling plantain and purslane
from the fresh soil around her sister
Evelyn's grave, my mother.

My father in the grey grass
takes a large wad of gum from his
dust-dry mouth — an effect of levodopa
without which he cannot move.
He tries to throw the gum away.
The wind throws it right back.

It catches in his fingers, cleaves to his shirt
sticks to his hair, forms skeins upon
skeins that entangle and entwine
until his fingers seem spinnerets and he
a spider becoming a fly
a prisoner in a web created by
wind, spirit, breath, air
or the gods of East Wawanosh.

From her knees, my mother
looks up at me — *I don't know
whether to laugh or cry.*

*— Mom, remember when Graham and I
were young, how, if we pleaded
hard enough for gum,
Dad would cut a Chiclet in half and
Graham and I would fight
over the little white crumbs?*

She leans her head against her sister's
tombstone. Her mouth opens, shoulders
shake — *Oh life. I never thought
it would be like this.*

xviii. Before

letter from my brother, 1

First act of retirement and I've made my largest capital acquisition of the year, a new, old-style scythe with a white ash wooden handle, almost extinct in this part of the world for several decades. Tried out the new scythe for a good part of the afternoon, mainly on goldenrod and milkweed but also thistles and burrs.

We have not had a usable wooden-handled scythe here at the farm in over forty years, and that long gone scythe was likely acquired over one hundred years ago. Following that, we had a number of aluminum-handled scythes, much too light to handle a heavy bull thistle, and the handle quickly bent, and soon after the blades fell out.

One can barely find any kind of a scythe in today's mechanized weed-eating world. The only one I'd seen was in St. Jacob's; it was fit only to hang on the wall as an antique. When dad was alive, and once fencing was done in the spring, he would send me to the back section of the farm, which wasn't tile drained as it is now, where I would cut with the scythe a whole field of Canada thistles. Once electric fences came in, I scythed the weeds beneath, so they wouldn't short out.

There are few men in North America now who know how to swing a scythe to best advantage, saving oneself to swing all day, yet cutting as many weeds as possible on every swing. I never thought I would be so greatly contented to own a scythe of old. Virtually $170 but no gas expense required, just elbow grease as dad would have said. And a $10 carborundum to sharpen the blade. None of the young clerks in the Wingham hardware store knew what I was talking about, but I persisted until they called the older proprietor, who happened to be in the back room. He found this scythe in the attic, said he had not sold one in years.

A real treasure for me, but will anyone appreciate it or even know how to use it after I'm gone? Our ancestors — especially Armand, Uncle Charlie and Dad — would be proud.

xix. Before

letter from my brother, 2.

There is nothing like slipping silently down a snow-covered road in the deep winter countryside behind a powerful steady horse — especially when swaddled in a buffalo robe.

I had forgotten how silent the cutter is; all one hears is the hooves as they slide along and of course the bells jingling.

I headed out the long lane, Delight in the harness, turned left and went down to the bridge, left again and we silently flew along the sixth line. We scared a huge hare who went bounding across the field in great leaps. Seeing neither car nor human, we decided to keep on, sailed straight through at the corner, past Uncle Charlie's place and down to the second bridge.

I had forgotten how much lower one sits in a cutter as compared to a cart, carriage or buggy, how much further back you are from the horse. The lines, reins for a rider, were almost too short! I thought about how my forefathers had voyaged down this same road in the same cutter so many moons ago.

The only part of me that was cold was my right thumb, due to a hole in my glove. I was wearing my worn blue shirt, long under-wear and several other layers, some that belonged to our father, some to Uncle Charlie.

The bridle that Delight wore was given to me by Uncle Charlie when he retired from farming in 1975. The bridle had hung in his attic ever since he gave up driving horses and bought his first car; the bridle had been down the sixth line as well, long, long ago. I found myself weeping like a child for the past.

xx. Before

Mother. Beyond your window, clouds
unrolled themselves to sheet-like flatness.
Your face, the pillow case, the walls — everything white.
You will be fine, you said, *your sister will be fine
but I ask you both
please to look after your brother.*

And while your request came after
his divorce and those estrangements
it was
before his daughter's suicide
before he went three-quarters blind
before he was struck by lightning
before the foal that was his daughter's namesake
was killed by lightning
before Parkinson's
before the octuple bypass
before he became estranged from almost everyone
before he refused ever to leave the farm
refuses, even now that the disease
freezes him, sometimes for hours
even now that he lives in a long shirt, because a long shirt
is all he can get on by himself.

xxi. Soft with the Horses

It snows and snows and snows. *Lake effect*
the weather says. Huron merciless
as God on Job, I say. My brother says
he got soft with the horses — allowed them
to stay in the box stalls — this means
fighting through drifts the size of cars
to carry pails of water from house
to barn. He is alone, in the snare
of the same disease that destroyed
our father, this work barely possible.

Yesterday's water froze in the night
he says. He dragged the heavy pails
back to the house, thawed the water
carried them to the barn a third time.
Forked manure, fed oats, fed supplement
fed flax. Curry combed their coats
picked up their feet to check them.
Bedded the seven horses deeply in straw.

The next night I phone again. Even colder.
He stokes the fire, discovers ice in the taps.
The ancient furnace on its lowest setting
runs almost continuously. No insulation
in the old house he refuses to leave,
holes the size of horse buns let in snow.
Drifts now the size of pickup trucks. He scrapes
the bottom of the barrel for peanut butter.
His bread supply reduced to stale crusts.
He cannot get soft with himself, he says.
He must make do.
Must leave his sons the largest legacy possible.
His father's rule.

xxii. Armand's Bed

Mother. We have done our best.

We have said, Let's take some of the money
from the sale of the horses and
buy a hospital bed with a back that moves up and down.

No, he says. I can't get rid of Armand's bed.

We can move Armand's bed to a different room.

We can't move Armand's bed out of Armand's bedroom.

Mother, you know that he likes to be addressed
in French. *Mon frère*, says my sister, *mon chou
écoute-moi, je t'en supplie.*
Armand was born in 1883.
He died in 1983.
His bed is at least one hundred years old.
It has the look of an animal who has given birth so often
its womb drags on the ground.
You never stop complaining about your back.
It's not Armand's bedroom, it's your bedroom now
and some days you can't get out of bed.

It's Armand's room, and it's Armand's bed.
We're not moving Armand's bed.

And Mother, everything is Armand's bed.

xxiii. No One

No one
can help my brother.
Everyone
who has tried to help my brother has said this.

Still, I thought I could help my brother.

There are Sundays that grow longer and longer and thin into
the shape of a snake
that twists itself around

your neck and tightens until you feel you might
strangle
especially when you are alone.

I began to phone on Sundays to give him
my listening
and by the end of the hour I would hear from him

a different voice, more breath beneath,
a tone with hills and valleys
no longer flat.

*

This past summer, half an hour into
a Sunday call
he took a sudden sharp turn: I hate your guts,

I will never forgive you.
Said this
half-weeping, half-shouting, voice shaking.

Ten years ago, just before his daughter's
funeral began,
his estranged wife had handed me a note

requested that I read it when
called upon.
It was a suicide note.

When the minister signalled me
I went to the pulpit and read the note.
No one, my niece had written

no one could have helped her.
No one
could have done anything to stop her.

My brother sobbed into the phone
that he had not known
there was a note

that shock, shame and horror
entered him —
to hear it read aloud to hundreds —

that the strength in his arms and legs
left him. Otherwise
he would have gone

to the pulpit, he said, wrapped his hands
around my neck and
strangled me.

Past a lump in my throat that felt like
a gravestone
I squeezed the words — I didn't know

either, just did what was asked,
at the last
minute. This was ten years ago!

It's today for me, he said.
It was your place to tell me.
You Are My Blood.

How could your blood tell you anything
that dreadful day?
I had no idea you didn't know.

My brother smashed his rotary phone into its cradle.

*

I have not phoned my brother, now, for two months —

thinking   thinking

*

No one can help my brother.
Everyone who has tried to help my brother
          has said this.

How can I help my brother?

His life is eating him from the inside.

Where shall wisdom be found?
                              And where
is the place of understanding?

xxiv. Sister Brother Sister

More and more often our brother becomes
without warning
a frozen figure of Pompeii
preserved at the second of his death,
a death that endures for longer and longer
periods. Yet
he will not, cannot, leave the farm, cleaves to it
as a man about to go to war
cleaves to his woman.
His adversary the same as our father's.
James Parkinson called it the shaking palsy.

My sister muses about assisted death.
I say it's unethical
for this suggestion to come from
anyone but him.

She says he needs to be
"cognitively intact"
for permission to be given. If it's left to him
it may be too late. My sister my best friend.
I know she's speaking from her doctor self.

Don't suggest it, just please don't, I say.

She says that she'll set fire
to the farmhouse
once our brother is gone.
The filth the rodents the bats the ruined roof the mold
that's eating the wallpaper.

I say that when I push open the door
to the back porch, its familiar *screak* over cement,
when I smell rubber boots, manure, old wood,
ashes and the hard-packed earth of the cellar floor,
it's the smell of home.

xxv. Forgiveness

*— Quotes from Shakespeare that enter the speaker's mind
are taken from passages that her brother could, at one time,
recite in their entirety.*

My brother phones, says he's decided
to forgive me.

*When thou dost ask me blessing, I'll kneel down,
And ask of thee forgiveness*

Says he's going to forgive me
because he's going to die soon.

*so we'll live,
And pray, and sing, and tell old tales, and laugh
At gilded butterflies*

Says he is falling every day and knows he will fall
into the wood stove and get burned badly enough
to die.

For in that sleep of death what dreams may come

Says he fell against the kitchen door jamb and hit his head
hard and saw stars.

Two of the fairest stars in all the heaven

Says that sometimes he cannot make the mouse
respond or press the keys

not a mouse stirring

Says that I am like the Amish, that I am insane and stupid and
a crook and parsimonious and a spy

as if we were God's spies …

Says not to email him, says my emails are too long, I am
wordy.

My words fly up, my thoughts remain below

I say that everyone is very worried about him, out there
all by himself on the farm.

He says that's hard to believe, as no one
ever phones him.

I say that if he's not nice, people won't phone him, that no one
likes to be called insane and stupid and a crook.

He says that I'm his sister, so he can say that.

Blow, winds, and crack your cheeks!
Rage, blow!

xxvi. None of Us

Father. At your funeral we meet an ancient ghost
cane and tremor, fluff and shadow —
    I went to school with him, you know.
    He helped the rest of us, taught us;
    your father was brilliant.
    And he beat up the bullies.

None of us had known.

My sister and I lift the lid of your coffin
just enough to see you. Your hands folded,
your hair still blond, your blue suit.
We say we are sorry, tell you that our eyes
are coming clear at last.
We say that you are free, now,
to work all day
in the fields. Elysian this time.

xxvii. Still

Mother. I want you to know
that you can still see Huron's stripe of dark blue
from the top of Carlow Hill
that the gulls still fly inland to the furrows
that the big hill still protects the house, that the valley
still deepens all the way to the creek
that the Red Maples still give up their sweetness in March
that your sister's son still tenders the sap
through wooden spiles he makes from sumac
still cooks the sugar water down
in cast iron kettles over an open fire.

I want you to know that the frogs still sing and sob
from the pond in spring, that the daffodils
around the foundation of the first house
still turn the west field yellow in April
that wild strawberries still glint from the grass in June
that the Mock Orange still arrives as a perfumed bride
at the beginning of July, that the salmon
still leave the lake for the Maitland River
still leave the river for the creek and spawn here
in the valley between the two farms.

xxviii. Huron County

Beets, borage, chunks of pork sausage, beef.
Horseradish on the side. Beer.
Huron County fare.

The river hopped up, run over. Gus not allowed
near. Dave and Doris honking to come see
their new red car.

Everyone runs out. Beet-red tongues, backs turned on Gus
who bounds toward the swollen waters
cuts himself

on a sharp stake near the bank, shoddy job by the beavers
who felled the tree. A high-running
stream of blood, then.

My sister is telling this story to our folks, assembled to meet
my daughter's new husband,
across whose visage

has trembled a cloud, white at first, darkening as sister says
she staunched the blood with tea towels, thought
they could finish dinner, but

the wound bled through, soaked the floor. A disturbance
of new husband's brow, a flicker of lightning
when sister says

she could have given anaesthetic herself, but there was no one
to stitch Gus up. Zigzag of new husband's breath
at daughter's ear.

Gus is a *dog*, says daughter, and all the maws open, guffaws
fall out, each re-hearing the story
as new husband

heard it — a redneck cesspool of borage and horseradish and
ruthless beavers, a child left bleeding
on the floor in tea towels

so that every beer could be quaffed, every last scrap of rare
beef gobbled — everyone laughing
but me as I watch my new

son-in-law to see whether he feels mocked, his new family
laughing at his expense, or whether he
can laugh too.

For an instant I see my daughter's future
happiness
hanging opaque

over
the swollen river, then
he laughs, and all Huron County rings with its light.

II

The Lives That Surround Us

Cairo Songs

Trips on the stairs of her daughter's walk up
trips on decorum, trips on her long black dress
climbs the up and up stairs of the endless walk up
necklace and dress and songs in her head
the smell of years, of thousands of meals, smear of the years
on crumbling walls, up, up and up until legs turn ancient
ancient stones of the Cairene desert, smells that meld
but are never done, the dogs of Cairo
know every one,
every bean, every sauce, every chunk of dark aubergine
dark as the swarms of locusts, the sandstorm skies, the blackbird eyes
of the men in the Cairene souk.

Replete with decorum her long black dress
red chains and red berries and brown cradle moons
brown cradle moons their suns split in two
necklace and dress and songs in her head
brown cradle moons and blackbird eyes, the blackbird eyes
of the men in the souk
how the eyes fly to her long, light hair, blackbird eyes
that pick off her hair
she twists her necklace its suns split in two
along comes a blackbird, she covers her hair
keeps track of the eyes in the Cairene souk.

A driver named Ashrab and songs in her mind
songs in her mind as he drives her home
songs in her mind and songs on his phone
driving her home from the Cairene souk,
four songs on his phone, the song of wife one,
song of wife two, the song of wife three
song of his business —
four songs on his phone
the phone that he answers while driving her home
five rows of traffic in three lanes of road, four songs
in her mind, one inch between bumpers, one inch

from disaster, eighty miles an hour, perhaps even faster
songs in her head on his phone in the horns,
the horns are a chorus, the horns are a language
he understands
he lives with wife three, *My Heart Will Go On* her song
in this land, in this land
where the clothes for the head are a song —
the Hijab, the Niqab, the Burka, the Shayla —
this land
where the q is not married to u
and a man may be married to many.

Thoughts at the End of a Lake Huron Pier

Last week, on the shore of Lake Huron, we said goodbye
        for another year to our daughter.
                A merciful sun looking straight into our eyes.

Our daughter lives near the Dead Sea, a salty prehistoric lake
        almost one thousand feet deep. On its west
                Israel and Palestine, on its east, Jordan.

When she was young we filled our daughter with love.
        From the parietal bones of her skull to the metatarsals
                of her feet, we filled her.

The idea to give her so much love that she could thrive
                                without us.

Back then, the books we read recommended this.
        Raise children to be independent. Leaving family behind
                means you've grown up.

The salt water of the Dead Sea is denser than
        a human body. Any movement is difficult.

A weak swimmer floating on his stomach in the Dead Sea
        may not be able to raise his head
                or turn himself over.

Many have drowned face down in the salty brine.
        I tripped on this fact only yesterday.

Last summer, a young man drowned right here at the end
        of this pier where I stand looking out on blue.
                The surface benign, the depths a roiling tide.

Before she moved to Jordan, our daughter walked down
        a familiar street in Montreal. Ten minutes later, an object
                fell from a crane. It killed a man
                        who walked where she had walked.

Once I knew that, the Middle East seemed safer.

And she has been safe, let me make that clear
      to me
she has been   safe.

So much blue out there. Blue the colour of feeling blue   blue
      the colour of looking back.

Lot's wife was forbidden to look back. She looked back anyway
      and God turned her to salt.

Our daughter. Back then, did we ever once consider
      whether we could thrive
                    without her?

Elizabeth Bishop said

that she was the loneliest person
who ever lived.

Ever. My heart skipped Double-Dutch when I heard that.

I've read many books on loneliness, placed them
        together on a shelf near my desk.

In an effort to wrestle loneliness and win
        I flew to Toulouse.
Went to Le Jardin des Plantes. Sat on a bench

told myself, No one within four thousand miles
cares whether you live or die.

Beneath my breastbone a rapid panic-flutter of flight feathers.

The story of Jacob wrestling with the angel flitting by.

In Le Jardin des Plantes are cunning
bridges, shaped
hedges, a Japanese garden.

How unexpected, then, the brood of hens
who appear at this moment
their familiar mindless bwa-a-a-ks and sudden outraged squawks.

My aunt used to take their sistren by the legs and
lay them on a stump and chop their heads off.

Yet here is this little flock at my feet.
They have turned their chicken cheeks.
Their wattles and their wing bows they comfort me.

sistren – extinct; former companion to brethren, which may still be
sighted in dense tracts

Chalazae

I tap two eggs against the bowl's rim, just the way
my mother did it. Two sharp, no-nonsense
cracks.

My mother removed the small white things
attached to the yolk.
Disgusted curl of her lip.

She thought them somehow impure,
stringy intruders that had wormed their way in
and sullied the sleek, shining yolk.

I, in turn, sever the "white things"
with a serrated knife, though I know they are only
small twisted ropes

that tether the precious sac of food
so it won't bang against the shell.
Chalazae.

Bits remain that must be fished and fished for
with a small spoon or sticky finger.
Each time I do this, I silently blame my mother

for this needless fiddling.
I think that way down
deep in themselves, many people

blame the mother, as if the various marks she made
upon our psyches and our somas
were indelible,

as if we were ultimately as helpless as the twisted
white chalazae
that slither under my knife.

Sudden Sweet Rain

He's painting the vertical posts of the fence
gray, she's on her knees
in the dirt, pressing Veronica
Spicata and Salvia Nemerosa
into darkness.
She's just told him their names
and they're laughing.
Spicata, she says, *Spicata.*
Her husband away on the other farm
hacking down thorn trees.

He's painting wood and
she's on her knees in soil and
a robin is joy of orange and shining flying
droplets above the stream.
He says that his mother
would have been seventy-four today.
Moving her hand's heel
around Salvia: *when did she die?*
Forty years ago today. Cancer.
How old were you?
Sixteen.

She walks to the pail and washes her hands
scrubs and scrubs at the dirt
beneath her nails: *That was tough.*

His face behind vertical bars of gray.
Me and my brothers
went wild. Crazy.
His tone matter of fact. No one
helped us. We were
altar boys. Not even the church
helped us.

A frisson of wind and the white
peony nearest the fence
makes sudden sweet rain.
It's the first time in the five years
they've been acquainted
that she's seen him
talk without working at the same time.

It was folly, all that came later, it was
folly, of course it was,
and looking back, she thinks
this was the moment it became
inevitable —
one of his work-ingrained hands
gripping the wet rail he'd just painted,
the other
idle at his side.

Hand

She refuses to take my hand today
though I've been picking her up
from school once a week. She stands
on the second step, face white
brows reshaped by a frown, dark eyes
fastened on distance, a figure
out of Margaret Bourke-White.
Does she want to make the cave
between chair and sofa? She will not
give me even her voice.
Our picnic of raisins and cranberries?
Will not look at me.
Can she show me her boots are not really
glued to the step?
Nothing. I sit down beside
her feet. The November wind blows up
a scuffle of wrappers and plastic bags.
The other children detour
around us, a few of the parents
send curious looks our way.
I look down at my hand on the step.
Gaze hard, as if I could see
the difference — the hand of a friend
become the hand of a stranger.
It waits beside her boots.

Heart

He paddles over, wearing that look you now recognize
      — guy with the story of why he's here
every day at senior swim. Scarce spikes of hair
and an eager smile, says his name's Carl
tells you right off that he is, not has,
a heart transplant.

You crouch in the shallow end, he places his chin on the rope
that divides you
says that twelve years ago an ordinary flu
      turned vicious,
travelled to his heart.

He looks at the water, then at you.

I would have died, but they sent me to a hospital
      that does transplants. There were
six of us, all men, all waiting for a new heart.

Carl tells you his story the way the Ancient Mariner told his,
as if he's been and perhaps still is "Alone, alone,
all, all alone,/Alone on a wide wide sea!"

He spreads his fingers, places his palm on the face of the water,
Sometimes I feel the lost lives here,
while I'm swimming.

Both of you look, then, toward the deep end as if
you might see
at least their shadows: that of the man whose heart
      now lives in Carl,
and those of the other five, the ones who died waiting.

Meine Einzige Blume

At first glance you almost seemed a *Weisse Fräulein*
from German folklore, a sylph of summer light
who floated from family room
to bedroom to sunroom.
Your bare feet seemed not quite to touch the silken blue beneath
but hover just above, though
as I came closer, I saw your hair, tangled and unbrushed
as if ready for a bird to take to the nest,
noticed that you held your arms out to the side
as if to balance your uncertain tack
through these rooms
you'd come to every year of your life for family times.
You touched the sofa, the bar, the table
all blue veins and unearthly pallor.
This was July.

It is said that a *Weisse Fräulein* may appear when a family
member is soon to die.
I remember this in late October
reading the eulogy to two hundred souls in pews
the eulogy your parents had composed.
Beyond the church windows, inklings of breath, spirit, wind
mauve clouds of somber mien.
As the day of your funeral wanes, I remember
an afternoon when you were five
how you sat on my lap as the winter light seeped away
had me repeat again and again
Du bist wie eine Blume — the whole poem —
and you learned, that day, to recite the first line.

From then on I called you
my one and only flower. *Meine einzige Blume.*

Weisse Fräulein — White Woman
Du bist wie eine Blume — You are like a flower
Meine einzige Blume — My one and only flower

Sitting

A chilly late-winter day in southern Ontario and Anusha has just
come around the corner wearing her *sari* and a winter scarf
wrapped like a *dupatta* around her head, her face older and sadder

than when I last saw her and she sits down on the cold
public sidewalk and looks up at me. Do I join her?
Given the weather and my age, an eccentric thing to do —

I don't care - in her culture it wouldn't be — but I'm not
in her culture — what will the neighbours think? I don't care
do I? She begins to talk and I sit down on the cement facing her.

Anusha's deep, dark eyes never leave mine as she tells about
the car accident, what her far-away children said
what the neighbours said, what the mechanic said, what the police

said, how the world looked that day, and every few minutes she slips in
her mantra *to cut a long story* — a bit of a question for me in her eyes —
will I rise and edge away or will I listen? I am listening

to the unwinding story and noting the drivers who twist their necks
to look at us, but at the same time thinking of my mother, who,
tired though she always was, would sit up late every New Year's Eve,

sit up late by herself, all the lights on, so that the neighbours
would not think that they — she and my father — were the only ones
who had no one to invite over for New Year's Eve.

Listening

It's the time of the first greening, the first warmth, the showing
of true blue Scilla, and I can't wait to work outside.

I've barely begun when Anusha appears in her mustard-hued *sari*
her worn face and sad dark eyes. Disappointment rolls down my limbs

like water, so ready they are for release by outdoor toil.
Anusha's stories are like the Ganges, she is apt to get lost in one or more

tributaries, to thrash her way upstream before slipping backwards
finding herself once again in the seemingly endless river.

Thirty years ago, Anusha's husband was my colleague. Every day
in a different silk turban — mint-green, melon, carmine, ivory.

An amiable man. We shared many laughs. We were ordering books
for the library the day he told me about the headaches.

Tests, and cruelly soon, the hospital. I visited him there. The bright
turbans gone, the silk suits. A straggle of long black hair

one eye bulging, one side of his body shrunken, the brain tumour
killing him quickly. His good hand gripped my left so tightly

that, for the length of the visit, the diamond I wore on that finger
cut and cut my flesh, red blood in a crease of the white sheet.

Too soon, the chanting of mantras, oil lamps, garlands of marigolds
the casket that held his body borne to the flames.

Screams of his small daughter. *Don't burn my dad, don't burn him.*

Today, my plans were to rake and prune, to haul heavy pails,
to undergo blood-letting by roses.

But the scar on the fourth finger of my left
hand reminds me. Sit down. Listen.

Eufrasio Says

that in his country, if your mother has died
she can stay in the ground
for two years and after that you must
come and dig her up, you must
dig until your shovel finds her coffin
six feet under the ground
and you must open the coffin.
The sun will enter first
then you will see a great emptiness
then dust and dirt and small insects
and at the bottom, bones, and that
will be your mother.

You must take the bones of your mother
out of the coffin and pour pure
alcohol onto a clean cloth and you must
clean and polish your mother's bones.
On some of your mother's bones
you will find small bits of flesh
that still cling. You must
separate them from her bones;
you will do this gently.

When you have finished cleaning
and polishing your mother's bones
you will be given a box
just big enough
to hold them. You will write
all your mother's names
on the box. The box will be filed
in a building made by the State
for this purpose and someone
newly dead
will have your mother's place
in the ground. If you wish

to visit your mother, you can visit
after you fill out a form
and wait for your day to come.

Eufrasio says that not everyone
is up to this work of digging up
his mother and even if you are,
you can be surprised by your own tears
coming from the bed you thought
was dry behind your eyes.

Coming to Canada i.

Then Kyra born in Greece tells us that her father
went to Canada and left them behind — her mother Marina
and four small girls —
left them with no money and said he would
send for them
and their mother worked in the fields ten hours a day
and left the nine-year-old to look after
her three young sisters
and their father didn't send for them
and their mother Marina kept them half-starved says Kyra
so she could save and save until she had enough
to come to Canada
and when she went to the ticket office with her four girls
lined up by height behind her
the officer said you can't go through unless you pay me too
and another man a stranger big and tall
stepped up and said you let her go through
and the officer let them go through
and when Marina got to Canada she found her husband
with another woman.

Kyra says that her mother's hair was black and stood out
around her head and her arms were huge and
strong and she said to her husband
you come back to your family or I'll kill you and he
came back and got a job washing dishes
but gave his money to his friends men friends
who needed money and called him a hero
and Marina found work cleaning houses though by then
she'd given birth to another girl and at last
a boy. She had a long pin and when the girls were bad
she pricked them.

Then Ivy says that her fate was decided by a long pin.
She and Ronny grew up in Manchester
and married in their late teens and thought they should

try Canada and a man in the pub placed a long
pin on Hamilton and said that place had lots of jobs
and when they arrived at last she said
they found *a knock up place*
on Barton Street and all the signs and all
the talk was in a language
foreign to them, Italian they later learned,
and they had almost no money and were hungry
and when they went out the first morning
the streets were full of little boys in green caps
who gave them shiny red apples
and nothing before or since
has ever tasted quite so good
and they wondered what place
they had come to
and they asked a man on the street
and he said *Yes, this is Canada.*

Coming to Canada ii.

Then Richard, who is eighty, says that his great great
grandfather Edmund came to Canada
from England after a rough passage of twelve weeks
and — in a letter to his brother dated 1832 —
said that he'd made his way to Huron Tract
where he planned to settle
and immediately lost to Cholera Morbus
his child Mary, then his wife, then his two youngest,
then little Edmund.
This the Almighty was pleased to send upon them
in the space of eight days and there was no one
but himself
to wrap them in the rinds of trees
and dig holes and lay them therein.
He apologized for sending this unpleasant account.
Said he planned to have a cow by next summer and
make his own butter;
he had no keep for a cow this winter.

Newfoundland Stories

i. Somebody Has To

Heather's Story

Smoke break on the balcony. Before us — the narrows the mountain the fog. I've been smoking since I was nine, Miss, but I'm down from three packs a day to one. Once, out there, the fog come up from the ocean like a finger; it looked like the finger of God, pointing.

I said to my mother once — why did you marry him? The two of you wasn't suited. She said, We had sex and I told the Priest and the Priest said When's the wedding? She lights another from the first. Deep drag. Chin up. I was the last of seven, the only one with dark hair and dark eyes. The runt of the litter. My mother put me on the street when I was thirteen. She said if she didn't, my father'd kill me. He used to beat me worse'n the others. It was because I looked like him, my mother said, and I was like him, and he couldn't stand it. When he got drunk, she said, he looked at me and saw himself.

I'm the one who looked after him. People say to me all the time, even my sisters say to me — how can you look after him after what he done to you, and I say, Somebody has to. He was what he was. People are what they are. He wasn't going to change.

He died on February 21st. This year, that's right, Miss. I give him breakfast, like usual, we had a good laugh over something and I went to the post office, and when I come back, he's sitting in his chair, but he's gone.

I have to move. I can still see him, sitting there in his chair, in my kitchen. I'm packing this weekend. I have to get out of there.

ii. A Barrel

Nellie's Story

Our men were trained to climb on the fishing boats and they went to New York City and worked in construction and they were called *The Fish*. The women went too. There'd be a family of thirteen and all the men would go, and all the women but one would go, and she was the one to stay home and look after the parents. My mother was *the one who stayed*.

The women cleaned the big New York houses in spring. The mistress of the house threw out the clothes she didn't want and the women saved them and shipped them in a barrel to Newfoundland and on Sunday a woman and her daughter would turn up decked out in finery and everyone would whisper behind their hands, She's got a barrel. It wasn't something you'd ever say out loud.

iii. Cellar Dwellers

Mary's Story

Louie and I are a new couple. Mrs. Doutney lived beside us and Mrs. Shambles lived beside her, and Louie lived in the next house. I've known him all my life. We're not married. We're living in sin. We're cellar dwellers. I had a full time job at Costco. I've just retired, and I did this Bed and Breakfast too, all these years. You won't see us by day. You'll have the house to yourselves, once breakfast is over. Folks like to be private. There's one exception. You'll see Louie every night on the stroke of eight. Louie insists on getting the coffee in the filter and pouring in the water the night before. There may be another exception. The house has a ghost. Sadie. You might see her. She's in a wheelchair. Your friend Linda's bedroom door opens outward and your friend Dick's opens inward — that's so Sadie can go smoothly from one room to another.

iv. Litany of the Saints

Mary's Story

I grew up in Harbour Main. Whatever was left over, my mom put out in the yard. She fed the crows and the dogs and the gulls. They all got along — there was never any fighting in the yard. The streets are empty now.

Willie Dugan died first, in December. He was a fourth degree Knight of Columbus and he organized the card games. He wasn't old, but he never had good health. Willie died and then Mrs. Nell Hickey died and then Mrs. Ursula Cavanaugh died and then mom died. After mom died, Nellie Sullivan died and after she died her friend Dish died — her real name was Mary Woodford but everyone called her Dish — and then Leo Woodford died (no relation) and then Father Heal died. That was his real name — Father David Heal. Father Heal said the prayers for Leo Woodford and he got as far as the funeral home porch and he collapsed and he died.

That's the end of it, for now. We haven't been out there for a wake since. People got to talking, when the old people went one after the other like that. It's Willie Dugan, they said, gathering enough folks for the cards.

Looking Out

It has been said that a pilgrim becomes addicted to the horizon
that semi-mythical distance we all know we can
                    never get to
                            that line we can never cross.

Many people make a pilgrimage to a great lake in summer.

The man who every day wears dark clothing in this heat,
has he come to absorb through his eyes and his ears
the rhythm of grief —
                whelm of engulfment
                        the reliable wane?

The woman in the straw hat who sits on the grey bench
                every morning looking out.
Perhaps she's allowing
            the trance of just being
                        to subsume her.

What happens when you spend time
                            on the edge
of such power, such beauty, such
possibility?

The longer I stand looking out, the smaller I become.

This morning, an expanding light that begins on the horizon.
Bright and wide as our vision, coming toward us across the big water.

Toward us or perhaps for us.

A light that makes you understand why
                          they were once *sore afraid.*

The Rules

The day, crisping up around me.
     Push the heavy snow, scrape the ice.
Think about my neighbour, right next door, his heart attack.
Imagine myself post heart attack
    in a scintillating silver gown
        among the Heavenly Host,
mouth a perfect O as taught by
                Mr. Attridge in grade four.
    My neighbour steps outside
to whisk — slowly — his car. Unsteady, face pale.
I lean on my shovel to listen.
           Learn that the pain
moved from left to right, that it
had him on the floor, that when it
moved to his back, it felt like
a bad boy
    hitting him with a baseball bat.
That he was in a cold sweat.

That they all gave him aspirin — wife,
ambulance attendant, fireman. That only
the fireman told him
          it must be chewed.
Why, I ask, did the ambulance sit in our street
for twenty minutes, him inside?
           There was only one
attendant, he says, the other had called in sick;
they had to wait for the replacement.
Rule: one cannot drive an ambulance to hospital
leaving the sick person unattended.
I ask my neighbour
        Isn't "unattended and on the way
to hospital" better than "attended while dying
in a stationary ambulance"?
My neighbour says he kind of thought that too
but didn't like to say.

Gordon's Bed

"for he counteracts the forces of darkness"
— CHRISTOPHER SMART on his cat Jeoffry

There is, of course, the story of the princess who lay upon
a stack of mattresses, her sleep fitful due to the pea
beneath the bottom layer.
There is the flying brass bed of Mary Norton's
imagination. John and Yoko upon their bed of protest
in Montreal, the long black locks that framed
their youthful faces, the white purity
of their clothing.

And there is the bed of my friend Gordon.
I have known him only as a widower, for the past
ten years his sole domestic companion a stocky
black and white cat named after Christopher Smart's
cat. Jeoffry waits for Gordon at the window
follows him from room to room like a dog.

Evenings, Gordon can be found in his unmade bed,
a bed remarkable for its bedfellows.
Books. Open, closed, new, used, crumbling, cat-eared,
proliferating. Books, and *The New York Times*,
Maclean's, *The Walrus*, *The Globe and Mail*, *The New Yorker*,
Scientific American, *The Literary Review of Canada*,
Harper's; there is barely room for Gordon and Jeoffry.

This night, Gordon is in bed as usual, immersed
in the unparagraphed mesmeric winding stream
of W. G. Sebald. In bed with Sebald, the written word
and Jeoffry, his subliminal purr,
the steady rise and fall of his feline being —
pneuma, spirit
                    invisible, immaterial.
Gordon closes his eyes to savour and stretch the moment
and the thought comes to him, then,
as the gentle tap of a friend:
This is my last domestic arrangement.

New Year's Day 2017

We had become accustomed to a muffled life, a life
without harsh shadow,
woolly whites and greys, roll upon roll of
cumulonimbus.
Suddenly this morning, the sun, as if
it had never been away.
The silence eerie, every branch still,
not a car moving from its driveway, not one person
walking on the sidewalk. Simply
this all-seeing orange eye that seems
aware of every disaster —
famine and drowning migrants and dying species
and children bullied into acts of desperation,
to name only a few.
All day the sun moves slyly across the sky as if
not to waken the slumbering.
It seems a god slipping across the world, a god
who believes the people are
asleep
to what is happening,
a god taking one last look around
before moving away from this planet for good.

Every Evening at this Time

In the condos that are
                          where the jungle once was
it is happy hour.
You think that it is happy hour
for the birds too; they are louder than
the drunks on the deck of the catamaran
that has just returned
                          from a day tour of the ocean.

You're not sure why you come here every evening
when the sun is mere fire at eye level
to sit beneath this tree
where the birds meet for a raucous, tropical yawp
and not just one kind of bird, many species
who fly in from all directions.
You tilt your head back to look at their varied shapes
mostly you just sit and listen.
You've heard that if you listen long enough
to a foreign language, it may begin
        to make sense.

Tonight, the birds' incessant chatter
                          reminds you
of your own aunts and grandmothers
their unabridged henhouse gabble, how, no matter
who was mad at whom
no matter how low the price of eggs or milk had sunk,
there was always
this discordant, aural comfort in the background.

Taking Stock

At the next table the Spanish ripples on
   over coffee and toast
that recurring sound, part burr and part trill.
   The sea, silver this morning.
Song after song of love
      the drum beat of loss.

Yesterday, in the pool's long blue
   you turned your head every
second stroke for a mouthful of sun.
   Today at this table you wait
for news of a loved one
      far away.

Last night at the restaurant down the beach
   the dishes were empty, the sea
speechless, moon a fragment of self.
   But we have the wine and the stars
said the owner.
      It is enough.

Here at this morning table you have
   star-fruit and mango and guava.
Coffee. You have your waiting
   and your worry and the sea
coming and going. Surely this too
      is enough.

In the space of ten minutes

two small woodpeckers trying so hard not to fall off
    the rough limbs of the lilac that their taps
        are ineffectual, beaks bouncing off the branch

a speckled mini-robin transfixed on a patio stone
    gazing at itself in a puddle

a baby grackle teetering on the birdbath edge
    so long that its mother flies down
        slaps him off with her wing

a thin sparrow open-mouthed on the fence
    parent placing a shiny black seed in the gape

A crazy surge of love for these baffled
    and befuddled creatures …
        I must have come outside

the moment after a host of mothers
    ejected their young from the nest
        perhaps a day or two too soon.

The Lives that Surround Us

Mange with its torturing itch
has destroyed his fur all the way to his haunches.
I put on my glasses.
Skin blue-grey, his left eye glassy, right eye dull
and half-closed. His once luxuriant tail
a ragged scrag of gristle.
He raises his small dark nose to the icy wind
sniffs and sniffs
digs in the hard mound of snow on the porch ledge
finds two cores with plenty
of wormy flesh. Saws them into himself.
Hunches his back against the sheltering brick wall
faces a weak glimmer of winter sun.
Tilts his head back
moves his paws on the little fur
left on his face.
I see with disbelief that he is grooming himself.
A few seconds of pleasure
at the end of a short life in nature's teeth.

On Turning Seventy

Now it is autumn and the falling fruit
and the long journey towards oblivion.

— D. H. LAWRENCE, "THE SHIP OF DEATH"

Late November. Leaves fallen, nests exposed.
My birthday comes and goes.
The days of our years threescore and ten.
My life on borrowed time begins. What's
the interest rate on that?

Swallowing lives newly ended with my toast.
His fervour, her wisdom, their eccentricity
inventiveness, exuberance.
Where does it all go?

D.H. Lawrence says we should stow our cooking pans
aboard our ship of death, take along
little cakes and wine for the journey. Unwilling to let go
these accoutrements of our lives in time
though he knows they'll be irrelevant in eternity.

I don't blame him. Who ever goes on a journey
without packing something
if only a toothbrush and a book, who ever
thinks his mortal coil alone will be enough?

John Berger says that the living are the core of the dead.
We in time, they in timelessness. They surround us
I surmise, as the apple surrounds its seeds.

Billy Collins says the dead are always
looking down on us as they row across heaven
in glass bottomed boats.
My mother was wise, perhaps, to leave
her eyes to science.

In Mexico, the dead return once a year on November 2nd.
The Day of the Dead — bigger than Christmas.
I guess *so*. If the dead of my family returned
I too would kill the fatted pig, roast it to succulence.

Oh, I know my mother (eyes restored
for this visit) would break her long silence with
"You look tired. You don't look
well. Oh, I don't think you've *ever* been well."
I'd open my arms, even to that familiar remark.
The long ache of her absence has changed me.

This same mother came back once.
A doubter, she returned from nine minutes of no
heartbeat a proselytizing Christian. She'd seen it all —
the radiant light, the tunnel, the loving presence
the whole scenario familiar from talk shows.

Brain scientists explain it away. My anxious mother
returns from death radiating peace.
The implications of each jostle within me.

We in time, they in timelessness.

John Donne says, *One short sleep past, we wake eternally.*
This the reverse of how I've always looked at it.

And yet, a dog hears more than we ever could
a hawk sees more, our senses puny by comparison.
Why do we think we know what lies beyond?

I have my own questions — how do I leave behind the scent
released by a broken tomato vine?
How allow the orange of the spring poppy to vanish
forever, its eyelashes and dark heart?

How forget the first note of the *Goldberg Variations*
all that it holds and foreshadows
how let go of the moment it entered the sun-shafted air
of Glenn Gould's funeral?
How let the memory of my infants' fontanelle slip away,
the way it pulsed beneath my fingers?
How stop naming and naming the particulars
of this life in time?
How feel anything but *rage*
against the dying of the light?
I predict my own *fierce tears*
will be the waters that bear me away.

They say that hearing is the last to go.
I trust there will be someone at my shore to prepare
my ship of death. I trust they'll read aloud
some of the poems I've quoted here,
then stow them all aboard.

I hope I don't have to choose between the poems and
the little cakes and wine.

Pelee Island

His hair is white, his eyes above the mask
   dark brown. One spark left.
He lifts his drill. Says he still hasn't

found himself. Says, *Do I want*
   to find myself? Might not like what I see.
She stays his drill, risks sounding like

a know-it-all, *That's part of finding yourself*
   — *remember Prospero*
'this thing of darkness I acknowledge mine.'

He says he wonders why he's never been
   to Pelee Island, as if it were
the unnamed island in *The Tempest,* as if

his unfound self were there, dangling its cold
   toes in Erie, waiting all these years
for its *temenos* to show up.

She says she's never been there either. He bends
   and whispers *Let's go together.*
She laughs, he laughs, but both desire

to shuck their roles, step out of
   time, abscond
to a Tempest-like place where

mystery lives, strange musics haunt the air
   spirits inhabit the forest
and they go looking for the dentist's Caliban.

Perfection

It rained and rained and rained. Then heat.
  And after all these years of toil for nought
or not enough, what I see today is mete
  and right. Nothing is perfect, yet this is.
Even the beetles black and golden
  in Gertrude Jekyll's whorls
seem perfect; I half expect them
  to roll onto their backs and wave
their thin legs in happiness, as a dog does.
  The beetles feed on the roses
as the ruby throat feeds on the orange trumpet
  of the vine, they feed as the robin
who yanks and yanks then rises with the worm
  they feed on the roses as the monarch
feeds on the Emperor Buddleja, those
  pointed purple sugar cones.
Early Girl and Brandywine have grown so high
  and spread so far they are entwined
with Eglantyne despite her thorns.
  This too is perfect — tomatoes and roses
inseparable. A teenaged Hairy Woodpecker
  practises drumming on the elderly lilac
that has long since proven it can survive
  anything.
                    This year, the weeping birch,
seemingly dead, has risen to stretch her graceful arms
  above the compost in blessing.
O do not eject me yet!
  Hang a flaming sword above the gate if you must
but let me stay here in this garden walled by green
  until I too reach perfection.

Notes

ii. Father

"who had nothing to kick but his dog": quoted as remembered from the author's eighth grade history textbook (circa 1956)

iv. "Birth of Son and Heir"

In his wonderful memoir, *Speak, Memory*, Vladimir Nabokov writes that simply to be alone among butterflies and their food plants was to know time as a mirage of human creation.

viii. Call Answer

CKNX: In 1924, when there were only five or six radio stations in Canada, a local Wingham man, "Doc" Cruikshank, put together a radio transmitter from parts in his shop, leading to his creation of CKNX and making him a legend in western Ontario and in the Canadian broadcasting industry. CKNX was officially licensed in 1935, giving this small town of 3,000 souls the distinction of having its own radio station.

Lost Heir is a card game played by folks in the East Wawanosh area of Huron County and likely beyond, although I have not personally encountered anyone outside that area who knew it.

xvi. The Sabbath

Loyal to his adoptive mother's beliefs, our father would not work on the Sabbath. "For in six days the Lord made heaven and earth, the sea, and all that in them is, and rested the seventh day: wherefore the Lord blessed the Sabbath day, and hallowed it." Exodus 20:11. King James Version (all Biblical quotes are from this version.)

The first Crokinole board is said to have been made by Eckhardt Wettlaufer in 1876, in Perth County, Ontario.

xxiii. No One

The italicized quotation at the end of this poem is from the Book of Job, 28:12.

Thoughts at the End of a Lake Huron Pier
"Lot's wife was forbidden to look back."
The quote refers to Genesis 12:26, "But his wife looked back from behind him, and she became a pillar of salt."

Elizabeth Bishop said
"the story of Jacob wrestling with the angel":
The story can be found in Genesis 34 and in Hosea 12.

Meine Einzige Blume
The poem is *Du bist wie eine Blume* by Heinrich Heine.

Coming to Canada ii.
Edmund's first months in Canada were described to me by a friend, Dick Capling. The letter was written by Dick's ancestor, whom I have called Edmund.

Looking Out
"sore afraid":
The reference is to Luke 2.9, "And, lo, the angel of the Lord came upon them, and the glory of the Lord shone round about them, and they were sore afraid."

On Turning Seventy
"The days of our years are threescore years and ten." Psalm 90.10

"rage against the dying of the light", *"fierce tears"*:
Phrases are from Dylan Thomas's famous villanelle, "Do not go gentle into that good night."

Pelee Island
temenos: Used in Jungian psychology to mean a safe space, the word derives from the ancient Greek for "container."

Acknowledgements

Heartfelt thanks to Linda Frank, Dick Capling, Ross Belot and John Terpstra for their support, advice and friendship; to the seven Paisley poets — Paddy Chitty, Birgit Elston, Kim Gair, Laura Gillis, Pauline Hewak, Sandra Lloyd, Elizabeth Tessier — who meet monthly at my home; to those who work on behalf of the Hamilton Poetry Centre, and those who attend the monthly workshops.

Special thanks to Robyn Sarah for her fine work as editor, particularly in sequencing the poems, and to Marc Côté, publisher of Cormorant Books.

Thank you to *Hamilton Arts and Letters Magazine*, to the Hamilton Public Library, to Bryan Prince Bookseller and *The Hamilton Spectator* for past support of the Short Works Prize and to the Hamilton Arts Council for their writing awards program, all of which have repeatedly benefitted my work. Thank you as well to the organizers of Hamilton's Grit Lit Festival and to the organizers of the Lit Live reading series.

I am grateful to the editors of the *The Malahat Review* and *The New Quarterly* who have continued to support my work and have published some of these poems. Also to *The Antigonish Review*, *Grain*, *The Dalhousie Review*, to Karen Schindler's Baseline Press, and to David Zieroth's The Alfred Gustav Press.

To Marty Gervais and T.W. McKergow, always.

Love and gratitude to my family, immediate and extended (especially Dan Pilling and Marie Gear) and to East Wawanosh itself, the existence of which has had a profound and lasting effect on my life.

About the Author

Marilyn Gear Pilling lives in Hamilton, Ontario. Her roots are in the East Wawanosh area of Huron County, which has been a powerful presence in her life and work. She is the author of three collections of short fiction, most recently *On Huron's Shore* (2014), as well as six collections of poetry. Pilling has won or placed in forty-five national contests for poetry, literary nonfiction and fiction, and has received twenty local Hamilton awards in those three genres. Past president of the Hamilton Poetry Centre, she has read in Holguin, Cuba and in venues that include Harbourfront, the Banff Centre in Alberta, and the historic *Shakespeare and Company* bookstore in Paris, France.

Author Land Acknowledgement

I live at the head of a lake beside blue waters. I live on a narrow coastal plain between rock cliffs and blue waters. I live in a place where long fingers of blue water once stretched deep into the land. I live in a place where spring-clear streams rushed down the rock face that surrounds the coastal plain. I live in the old city of Hamilton, the part between the escarpment and the water.

Beautiful Waters was the name of our bay — Macassa, in the language of our first people. The rock cliffs we call the Mountain were dense with foliage. Green meadows undulated between the streams and the long, deep inlets edged with sword grass. Forests of virgin oak, maple, ash, hemlock and spruce were home to a Noah's ark of animals.

Every autumn, the forests gave up harvests of walnuts, beechnuts, chestnuts, butternuts, and hickory. Every dawn and every dusk, thousands of waterfowl gathered at the blue waters to drink and feed. The deer left hoof prints in the mud. The hoof prints filled slowly with water and turned to gold as the sun rested on the western horizon.

For ten thousand years, this place was as I describe. Generations of Indigenous people lived here in the primeval forests, beside the clear blue waters.

Then we white settlers came along. In two hundred years, we changed this place at the head of the lake into what we see now. We filled in the inlets, cut down the trees, paved the ground beneath our feet, polluted the water and the air, and drove away the animals. I am mindful that I live and write on the traditional territories of the Mississauga and Haudenosaunee nations, and within the lands protected by the "Dish With One Spoon" wampum agreement, and I am saddened by too many of the changes we have made in the past two hundred years.

— *Marilyn Gear Pilling*

We acknowledge the sacred land on which Cormorant Books operates. It has been a site of human activity for 15,000 years. This land is the territory of the Huron-Wendat and Petun First Nations, the Seneca, and most recently, the Mississaugas of the Credit River. The territory was the subject of the Dish With One Spoon Wampum Belt Covenant, an agreement between the Iroquois Confederacy and Confederacy of the Ojibway and allied nations to peaceably share and steward the resources around the Great Lakes. Today, the meeting place of Toronto is still home to many Indigenous people from across Turtle Island. We are grateful to have the opportunity to work in the community, on this territory.

We are also mindful of broken covenants and the need to strive to make right with all our relations.

Poetry from Cormorant Books

Undercurrents: New Voices in Canadian Poetry
(Robyn Sarah, editor, 2011)

No End in Strangeness: New and Selected Poems
(Bruce Taylor, 2011)

Some Frames (Jack Hannan, 2011)

The Other Side of Ourselves (Rob Taylor, 2011)

The Jonas Variations: A Literary Séance (George Jonas, 2011)

Ash Steps (M. Travis Lane, 2012)

Waking in the Tree House (Michael Lithgow, 2012)

Tilt (E. Blagrave, 2012)

The Port Inventory (Donald McGrath, 2012)

All the Daylight Hours (Amanda Jernigan, 2013)

A Bee Garden (Marilyn Gear Pilling, 2013)

A Rhythm to Stand Beside (Jack Hannan, 2013)

Hungry (Daniel Karasik, 2013)

Looking East Over My Shoulder (Jill Jorgenson, 2014)

When We Were Old (Peter Unwin, 2014)

Light Takes (Mia Anderson, 2014)

Crossover (M. Travis Lane, 2015)

Catullus's Soldiers (Daniel Goodwin, 2015)

Borrowed Days: Poems New and Selected (Marc Plourde, 2016)

Building on River (Jean Van Loon, 2018)

Giacometti's Girl (Sandra Davies, 2018)